The Creation Museum

Behind the Scenes!

AMAZING STORIES OF GOD'S PROVISION FROM CONCEPTION TO COMPLETION!

1:1

answersingenesis
believing it. defending it. proclaiming it.

Written by Stacia McKeever, Gary Vaterlaus, Diane King
Edited by Becky Stelzer, Stacia McKeever, Roger Patterson,
Gary Vaterlaus.
Cover design & text layout by Brandie Lucas & Diane King

ISBN: 1-60092-224-4

Printed in China.

Table of CONTENTS

Envisioning a Museum

A young boy stands in front of an exhibit at a natural history museum. His father points to the chimp-like skeleton called Lucy and exclaims, "Son, this is your ancestor!"

In front of the museum, children stream out of buses and file into the modern-day temple to naturalism, eager to learn the stories of an ancient earth and their ascent from a microbe via undirected evolutionary processes.

Around the world, natural history museums, like London's Natural History Museum pictured here, lead children and adults astray concerning the history of the universe and their place in it. The God-inspired account found in the Bible's first book, Genesis, is set aside and replaced by ideas based solely on human reasoning.

This book is the account of how a schoolteacher in an unlikely location was burdened to help set the record straight.

As a public school science teacher in Australia in the 1970s, Ken Ham (now president of Answers in Genesis [AiG]) took his students to these museums. Yet he was burdened when he saw the lies of evolution and millions of years of history become a stumbling block to the children, preventing them from even considering the Bible's claims because they believed it was an outdated irrelevant book filled only with nice, moral stories.

As he realized the false teachings permeated far beyond the walls of the natural history museums, reaching even into the local churches, his heart ached. His cry to the Lord became "Why can't we have a creation museum that teaches the truth?"

Ken Ham's parents, Norma & Mervyn Ham

1970s

Ken's father taught him to stand on God's Word. In the face of the liberal pastors of the day, his father continually defended the Bible, providing answers to the skeptical attacks on the Word of God. Watching his father, young Ken learned to stand up for what Scripture taught no matter what anyone else said. His father and mother cultivated in their children a deep love and respect for the Bible, teaching them that God's Word alone must be their final authority.

Ken saw the need to call people back to the truth and authority of God's Word, particularly in the book of Genesis, by providing answers to questions about the creation/evolution issue. In the early 1980s, Ken met accountant John Thallon *(right)*, who shared Ken's burden to see a museum that taught the truth about history based on Genesis chapters 1–11. Together, they knelt in prayer on a piece of property between Brisbane and the Gold Coast in Australia, asking the Lord to give it to them for a museum.

John Thallon

1980s

But God's ways are not our ways. He didn't grant the request Ken and John made concerning that particular piece of property. The Creator did answer, however, in ways that they couldn't even begin to imagine.

Over the next few years, Ken realized that Australia's small Christian population could never support such an endeavor. He also felt burdened that the key to reaching the rest of the world was to impact Christians in the United States of America. In 1987 Ken and his family moved to San Diego, California, to work under Drs. Henry Morris and Duane Gish at the Institute for Creation Research. Then in 1994, with the blessing of ICR, he and his family settled in Kentucky, only a few miles from Cincinnati, Ohio, a strategic location to the rest of the U.S.—within a day's drive of almost two-thirds of the U.S. population.

Ken and wife, Mally, with their children (mid-1990s)

1990s

Two books played a pivotal role in sharpening Ken's message about the truth of the Bible's account of history. The first was *Evolution: Science Falsely So-Called*, which emphasized that man's sin brought death and the need for salvation from sin (Genesis 3). Before the fall of man into sin, death had no part in God's original "very good" creation. And any attempts to insert millions of years of death, disease, and suffering (based on the fossil record) into the Genesis account destroyed this doctrine. The small book provided Ken with the theological answers he needed to counteract evolutionary and old-earth ideas. The second book, the *Genesis Flood*, provided Ken with scientific answers to the debate.

THE GENESIS
FLOOD

The Biblical Record
and Its
Scientific Implications

JOHN C. WHITCOMB, JR.
HENRY M. MORRIS

Answers in Genesis

With cofounders Mark Looy and Mike Zovath, Ken started the Bible-defending ministry, Answers in Genesis, bringing with him the ever-present vision for a creation museum. It was in Kentucky that Ken would see the realization of the prayer he had prayed so many years before.

THE CREATION BOOKSTORE

Ken Ham   Mark Looy   Mike Zovath

(1995)

This is the story of how a father and mother who teach their children to stand on the authority of God's Word can leave a legacy that impacts millions.

First potential property near Big Bone State Park

Mark Looy and Mike Zovath

Searching for Property

1996

March	Shelton land found
Aug. 28	Shelton rezoning public hearing—planning commission
Sept. 6	Land use issues—Big Bone controversy begins
Sept. 9	Committee meeting vote 4–0 in favor
Sept. 9	"Save our comprehensive plan" campaign with opposition (Concerned Citizens of Boone Cty.) to oppose AiG in packed courtroom
Sept .10	Disinformation campaign hits news
Sept. 18	Planning commission vote 9–4 in favor
Nov. 25	Fiscal court public hearing—packed house
Nov. 27	Ministry finances questioned; Ken attacked—headlines
Dec. 10	Fiscal court vote 4–0 opposed Genesis Park
Dec. 11	AiG seeks new property

1997

Jan. 12	Other land offered to AiG
Jan.	Ministry moves to Industrial Rd. location in Florence

1998

Feb.	New land found on Deck Lane (Petersburg)
June 24	Rezoning public hearing (to industrial)—planning commission
July 7	1st committee meeting
Aug. 6	2nd committee meeting
Aug. 19	3rd committee meeting 4–1 in favor
Aug. 19	Planning Commission vote 8–7 opposed, sent back to committee
Sept. 3	New committee meeting 3–2 in favor
Sept. 16	Planning commission 9–5 opposed

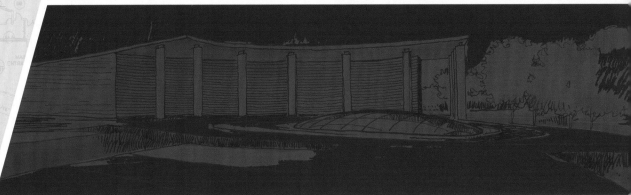

Creationists targeted
Opponents seek method to block museum

BY ANDREA TORTORA
The Cincinnati Enquirer

FLORENCE — They listened to scientists, clergy and attorneys offer opinions about evolution and why it should be taught.

the crowd.

"It's time to fight fire with fire," Carl Frye, of Walton, said. "We don't have time to talk about it. We have to move now."

Answers in Genesis, a religious group that promotes the biblical belief of creation, has

Creationist views will dominate museum

Dinosaurs wou[ld] [roa]m Noah's a[rk] [i]n one exhibit

[As]sociated Press

Museum opponents vow to fight

By Amy Charley
Editor

Neighbors who live near a proposed Creationist museum in rural Boone County say they're organized now and they will

Mike Zovath, AIG's general manager, said the Genesis Park presentation at Fiscal Court would be similar to the one given to the planning commission. He plans to take a few minutes to explain both the ministry

report details the project.

The ministry has already begun accepting donations for the project, although Zovath declined to say how much had

GANNETT NEWSPAPER ● 501,100 Readers Daily   WEDNESDAY ● DECEMBER 11, 1996   AN EDITION OF THE CINCINNATI ENQUIRER ● 35 CENTS

Boone refuses museum zoning
Creationists say they'll look for another site

BY TERRY FLYNN
The Cincinnati Enquirer

BURLINGTON — Despite Tuesday's setback in plans for a creation museum, the Christian ministry Answers in Genesis isn't leaving Northern Kentucky and probably will look for another site in the Boone County area.

"That was the indication from

Court members denied a request by the ministry for a zone change that would have permitted construction of the Genesis Park museum and the group's new office.

"We're not going anywhere," Mr. Zovath said of Answers in Genesis, which operates out of offices in Florence. "There is other property out there. This won't

Fiscal Court, by a 4-0 vote, denied AIG's request to change the zoning on 40 acres of a 97-acre tract off U.S. 42 south of Union. The group had planned a museum that would emphasize the Biblical view of creation, and also intended to establish a nature walk in addition to offices and a warehouse for the ministry's mail order offerings.

surprisingly upbeat after the fiscal court meeting.

"The first thing we'll do is enjoy th[e] ... land."   Ken Ham.   ▶ The religio[us]

new piece of

Inside/A12

Fiscal Court's decision." AIG can sue in Boone District Court for a reversal.

Genesis group seeks site
Creationism museum regroups

SUNDAY ● JANUARY 12, 1997

tive director said. "We thought we had the right idea before, but (Boone County) Fiscal Court changed that."

AIG sought a zoning map amendment on a 40-acre parcel

business, as well as walking trails and a picnic area for museum visitors.

"We want to stay in Northern Kentucky, whatever that may mean," Mr. Zovath said. "We

"We're going to ask (Boone) Fiscal Court what we need to do, to explain where our particular operation fits into the zoning regulations," he said. "Then we'll go out and look for that

decision."

He said the group has three or four options on what would be built.

He said AIG probably will look for 20 to 30 acres. "We don't

Creation museum gets national s[upport]

and park.

"This has become a very emotional, very sensitive issue, and has produced a tremendous amount of response," Mr. Costello said Friday. "We have received over 200 phone calls and many letters and faxes from all over the country."

Answers in Genesis, a conservative evangelical ministry based in Florence, is requesting a zone change on 40 acres at U.S. 42 and Rt. 338 near Union.

The Planning Commission held a public hearing on the request Aug. 28, where a number of people voiced opposition to the proposal. Most of those speaking against the Biblically centered museum did so for religious and/or scientific reasons. A few questioned possible traffic, drainage and sewer problems the park might create.

"The planning commission is looking at this request strictly from the land use issue, because

most all the phone calls and letters we've received deal with the religious aspect of the museum, not zoning and land use."

The museum, dedicated to the biblical interpretation of the creation, would feature dinosaur models, fossils, mineral displays and taxidermy exhibits. Offices, athletic fields and areas for wildlife observation and reflection also would be included.

More than 50 letters and faxes have arrived at the plan[ning]

Planners ignore report, reject museum

By Crystal Harden
Post staff reporter

Kevin Costello, executive director of the Creation museum, showed a drawing of the museum to the commission Wednesday.

Boone OKs rezoning plan
Post staff report

Committee votes 3-2 for creation museum

By Joe Christofield
Staff Writer

Judge rules for creation museum

Says decision on zoning was legal

BY KRISTINA GOETZ

Creation museum plea reheard

Supporters and foes at planning meeting

By Crystal Harden
Post staff reporter

Route that a zone change takes

Opponents of Genesis museum end battle

BY KRISTINA GOETZ
The Cincinnati Enquirer

BURLINGTON —

The Kentucky Post

JOSEPH HOWARD

Edition of The Cincinnati Post

© FRIDAY, MAY 7, 1999

Creationist museum appro

THE CINCINNATI ENQUIRER
KENTUCKY
DEN, 578-5555; FAX, 578-5565
WEDNESDAY • NOVEMBER 11, 1998

Ky. brie
Obitua
Busine

Genesis museum fails a

Boone board unanimous on rezoning

BY EARNEST WINSTON
The Cincinnati Enquirer

In 1995, the search for suitable land for the Creation Museum and new Answers in Genesis headquarters began in earnest. Ken, Mike, and Mark examined a number of properties.

The AM Kinney architectural firm produced the architectural drawings of the museum building and offices. They also donated a significant portion of the hours spent on the project as a contribution to AiG.

In March of 1996, AiG made an offer on what was called the "Shelton property," about 20 miles south of Cincinnati and four miles off Interstate 75, south of Florence, Kentucky. This 97-acre property was deemed a good site not only because it was close to the interstate, but also because its many trees and ponds would make it a wonderful site for a museum and nature park.

Before closing on the sale, the property had to be rezoned from an agricultural to a recreational/public facility designation. But by December of that year, after opposition from a local secular humanist group and others, the fiscal court of Boone County had voted 4–0 to deny the rezoning petition (even though the planning commission had recommended approval).

1997

After a lengthy search for the perfect piece of property, Answers in Genesis acquired the current property near Petersburg in February 1998. Then the process to rezone the property began.

> As always, God's ways are not our ways. He had a much better place in store for the Creation Museum.

Land found alongside I-275, just two exits west of the Cincinnati Airport

Can you hear me now?

One of the only visual drawbacks to the Petersburg property was the 250-foot cell phone tower that had already been built on the land and the accompanying easement road that ran straight through the center of the property directly in the path of the museum site. The upside is that anyone with Verizon service gets great signals throughout the museum!

Cows, horses, and a donkey were roaming this property when we bought it.

1998

It was an uphill, multi-year battle with the Boone County Planning Commission. In the midst of the struggles, AiG held a rally on the property to encourage our supporters (and the AiG staff!) on November 21, 1998.

AiG staff visit the property during fall of 1998

300 rally to support creationist museum

Group's legal action claims Boone bias

BY SUSAN VELA
The Cincinnati Enquirer

BURLINGTON — About 300 people gathered Saturday to support a controversial religious group and the legal action it has

Proposed site of Answers in Genesis HQ

of approval and agreed nance infrastructure for property, he said. Yet B County Fiscal Court mem and Boone County missio

The original land-use map, provided for the zoning request (*below*), shows a different-shaped building and parking lot and the cell tower easement by the lake. Permission was later obtained from Verizon to move the cell tower easement, which freed up additional space for both building and parking. To the right is one architect's rendering of the museum. This plan was obviously not used.

AiG was informed of a museum in Baltimore, Maryland, that was going up for auction. Without any knowledge of what the Creation Museum would need, the opportunity seemed too good to pass up. Most auction attendees were not interested in the actual exhibits, and AiG was able to purchase $5 million worth of exhibits for only $19,000. Among the exhibits purchased were a 54-ft. walk-through fish replica, a walk-through model of a living cell, and a 500-gallon marine aquarium. Only a few of the exhibits were used, but thousands of dollars worth of lighting and other specialty equipment found its way into the finished museum.

2000

Finally, after two long years of back-and-forth battles between committees, commissions, and the fiscal court (and a lawsuit that AiG won), approval was granted to rezone the property in March 2000. The property was purchased two months later. At the closing, Ken's dream of a creation museum became much more real. He stated:

> This is the beginning of a new era for creationism worldwide. Our family museum and center will be the first major creation/biblical history museum of this size anywhere in the world. It will be a legacy for future generations who will visit and learn about the message the Lord is entrusting to us today. This major outreach will stand as an incredible witness to the world that the Bible is true from its very first verse, including its message about the gospel of Jesus Christ.

About 250 people gathered on June 17, 2000 to dedicate the property to the Lord. Dr. John Whitcomb, coauthor of *The Genesis Flood* (the book that had so encouraged Ken over 25 years previously), prayed that the Lord would greatly bless the future museum and AiG headquarters. He also added that if the building complex were ever used in a way that would be dishonoring to Him and His Word, that God would remove it from the face of the earth.

On May 5, 2000, the papers were signed!

Ken Ham and Dr. John Whitcomb

After the ceremony, the visitors strolled the property and fellowshipped with AiG staff and Dr. Whitcomb. Several guests commented to Ken how thrilled they were to be a part of this historic event in the life of AiG and its proposed museum.

Although the property had been rezoned, the request for approval of the waste-water treatment plant had yet to be granted. This further delayed the commencement of the museum's construction.

Staff and friends gather to dedicate the property to the Creator!

Bringing the biblical vision of creation to life

2001

With the waste-water treatment plant decision still in the committee's hands and the site-plan approval in limbo, AiG gained approval to break ground on the property in March 2001. Freezing rain and a cold wind did not daunt more than 600 supporters who participated in the March 17 groundbreaking ceremony.

The 260 cars, parked in the muddy field, displayed license plates from several states, including Alabama, Illinois, Michigan, Missouri, Tennessee, and others. One AiG supporter, Mr. Elton Batchelor, drove all the way from northcentral Arkansas (more than

a 600-mile journey) just to be a part of this historic event in the continued battle for the authority of the Bible. And then we found that a Florida couple drove 14 hours to be with us!

The shovels were painted gold just the night before and were barely dry for the ceremony.

CREATION MUSEUM AND FAMILY DISCOVERY CENTER

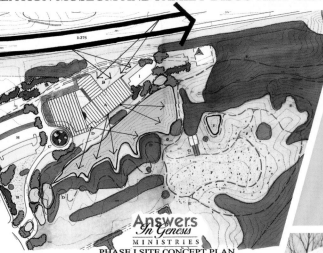

Answers In Genesis MINISTRIES
PHASE I SITE CONCEPT PLAN
PREPARED BY A.M. KINNEY AND MEISNER + ASSOCIATES
SEPTEMBER 2000

At the long-awaited groundbreaking ceremony, AiG unveiled its newest dinosaur model, sculpted by Buddy Davis. It was a magnificent 17-foot long, 10-foot high Stegosaurus that now resides in the museum's Dinosaur Den.

From left to right: Ken Ham, Mike Zovath, Ted Schulz, Mark Looy, Carl Kerby, John Pence

The day was so cold that most of the supporters huddled in the tent drinking complimentary hot chocolate, coffee, and tea.

Note the red line that shows the footprint of the finished museum and headquarters on the property. I-275 is on the left.

Constructing a Museum

2002

July 1   Water-treatment permit in hand; site plan approved
July 15   Rough grading completed; underground water/sewage lines started
July 22   Underground utilities in progress; asphalt contract awarded
Sept. 16 Foundation permit approved
Nov. 18 Northeast warehouse wall poured
Nov. 25 South wall warehouse work
Dec. 9   Building permit in hand; cold weather slows work

2003

Jan. 20 Final foundation walls poured
Jan. 27 Curved wall completed
Feb. 24 Weather delays postpone steel delivery
Mar. 3   Items brought down from Xenia, Ohio, to warehouse
Mar. 24 All screen walls poured; work on floor pads and steel columns
Apr. 7   Six loads of steel delivered
Apr. 14 Steel goes up
May 5   Two-thirds of the steel erected
May 12 Work starts on mezzanine footers
May 19 Digging elevator shafts
June 16 Work includes roof, elevator shaft, underground plumbing, and electrical
June 30 Floor slab for warehouse poured
July 7   Workshop slab poured; utilities complete; roof on workshop and half of museum

One of the verses Ken routinely uses to demonstrate the importance of establishing the proper foundation of God's Word is Psalm 11:3, "If the foundations are destroyed, what can the righteous do?" Even from his early days of sharing the message of biblical authority, Ken would point out that every biblical doctrine ultimately finds it foundation in the book of Genesis, and particularly its first eleven chapters. In other words, Genesis 1–11 is the history that is foundational to the rest of the Bible, and thus all Christian doctrine. This message comes through loud and clear in the Creation Museum.

And nowhere is this message better illustrated than with the foundations that were poured for the Creation Museum in October 2002.

Finally, after 25 years of waiting for God to fulfill his prayer, Ken knew that the Creation Museum was actually being built. As he and Mike stood in front of this fire hydrant on the property, Ken thought, "This is really happening!"

Site preparation begins summer of 2002.

A bulldozer was donated by a supporter in Washington state and taken on a 5-day journey to Northern Kentucky to help grade the museum property.

At all stages of construction, from graded land and roughed in walls, to the daily operation of the museum, this property has been bathed in regular prayer.

The house situated at the end of Deck Lane was another unforeseen boon. Purchase of this property removed several land-use concerns and was used as a construction office and later as a house for volunteers.

11-22-2002

Local resident Kevin Markesbery (*below*) left his job in the construction industry for two years to become construction manager of the Creation Museum building project. His experience and knowledge were invaluable in getting the museum built.

It was necessary to excavate more than 14 feet below grade.

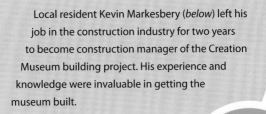

Artist's concept

BUILDING TIMELINE

As all good evolutionists know, change takes time. However, far more was involved in the construction of the Creation Museum than time and chance. This pictorial overview shows the progress from vision to completion in five years. Much prayer, creativity, money, and work went into the final Creation Museum than is immediately visible to the eye. Praise God for His goodness!

Designers chose stone pavers over cement for the public walkways in order to preserve the natural appearance of the museum.

1-9-2003   6-10-2003   8-29-2003

The Creation Walk, the centerpiece of the museum, was the brainchild of Patrick Marsh, museum design director. The original architect's plans called for a large open room and steps.

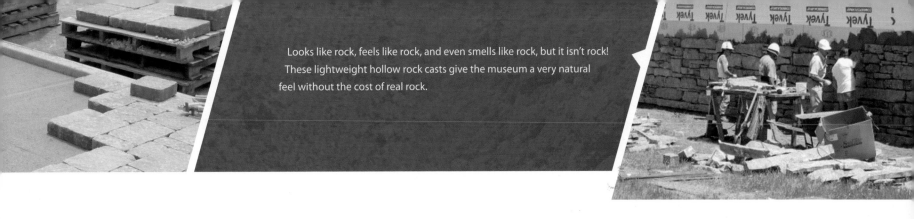

Looks like rock, feels like rock, and even smells like rock, but it isn't rock! These lightweight hollow rock casts give the museum a very natural feel without the cost of real rock.

11-12-2004   9-6-2006   1-19-2007

These trailers occupied the circular space in front of the museum for many months. They housed the construction office and the museum artists, who needed on-site access to the developing museum for the exhibit concepts.

WORKER LUNCH

The museum made strides toward fulfilling its mission long before the walls were even finished.

On February 26, 2004, Answers in Genesis hosted an on-site lunch for all the construction workers involved in the project, many of whom were not Christians. Each worker was given a booklet that gave a complete overview of the project they were working on, including the Seven C's of History and the plan of salvation. Worker photos were also included on the inside covers to make them feel a part of this God-honoring project.

The hearty lunch was well received, and many of the workers sat down and read the booklet cover to cover before returning to work.

Over the entire construction project, we know of at least seven workers and vendors who were led to the Lord through the witness of AiG staff and volunteers.

Each worker was given a custom witnessing booklet created for this one event.

It couldn't have happened without our wonderful volunteers! To give you an idea of the important role they played, during one eight-month period, more than 200 out-of-town volunteers put in more than 8,000 total hours of work.

Affectionately known as the Three Amigos, these gentlemen have been long-term volunteers for Answers in Genesis. From left to right: Al Barbieux (now with the Lord), Art Hunsicker, and Dick Sauer.

Gene Earnest, master woodworker

Marlene Sauer has volunteered since year one of AiG's existence.

HEADQUARTERS

An unnecessary loss of funds through rent on buildings in Florence, Kentucky, was eating into AiG's available funding. It made good financial sense to push to complete the ministry headquarters and get moved out of the four rented offices. In September of 2004, occupancy was granted on the ministry's new onsite headquarters. Staff moved in Labor Day weekend and were quickly back to work.

With everyone now on site, the project to complete the museum and the exhibits and grounds swung into high gear.

4-2-2004   5-5-2004   8-12-2004

The staff entrance

Mike Zovath, Ken Ham, and Kevin Markesbery

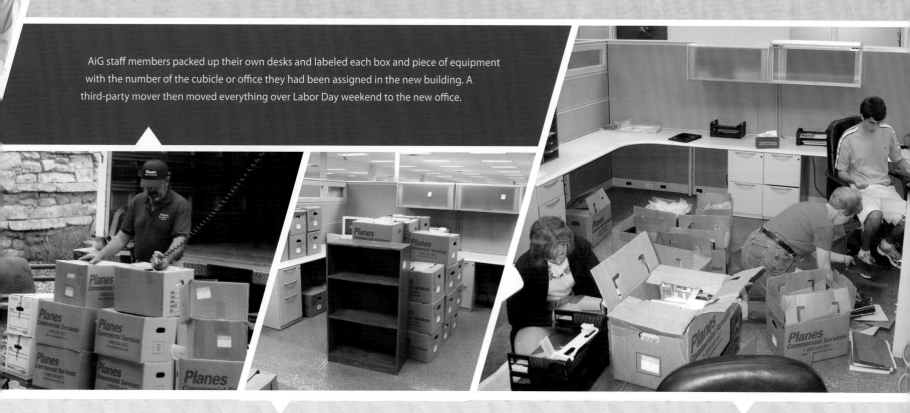

AiG staff members packed up their own desks and labeled each box and piece of equipment with the number of the cubicle or office they had been assigned in the new building. A third-party mover then moved everything over Labor Day weekend to the new office.

The mover delivered the boxes and equipment to the correct locations within the office, leaving them in neat stacks for future unpacking.

On Tuesday morning the unpacking began. Most staff members were able to get settled and back to work within the first day. After years in cramped and less-than-ideal working environments, AiG members staff praised God for their new office.

Jesse Pié works on a Pteranodon.

Filling the Museum

The two years before the Grand Opening, the museum saw constant activity as the landscaping progressed on the outside, and the exhibit halls were constructed on the inside. AiG staff, hundreds of volunteers, and outside contactors worked together to pave trails, plant bulbs, build walls, install tile, pull cable, build models, and mold mountains of foam into rocks, trees, and animals—all as the 2007 Memorial Day weekend deadline rapidly approached. Central to the task was a dedication to quality workmanship using the latest technology, and an unswerving commitment to biblical accuracy in every exhibit.

EXHIBIT DESIGN

Although Ken, Mike, and Mark had hired architects and project managers to complete the exterior of the museum, they were slightly at a loss as to how to fill it.

And then the Lord brought along Patrick Marsh, former scenic designer of the Jaws and King Kong attractions at Universal Studios in Florida.

Patrick brought with him the vision of making the museum more than stuffy exhibit halls filled with bones and fossils. He realized that in this day and age, an effective museum cannot be solely an attractive building with artifacts and text-heavy signs on the walls. In general, people do not read most of those signs and learn very little in such an environment. To effectively present a message, it must be designed and developed as "edu-tainment."

Realizing that such plans require more money, Patrick asked the AiG board to consider expanding the original budget of $14 million to $25 million. After much prayerful consideration, the board gave the go-ahead, and new plans were set in motion to make the Creation Museum a truly unique experience. Mike would oversee the construction of the museum and its exhibits, while Mark did the public relations and fundraising.

Patrick began building his design team, filled with sculptors, exhibit designers, illustrators, and jacks-of-all-trades. These folks began bringing the vision for the Creation Museum to life. Many often asked how AiG found these very talented people. Ken's answer, "Just as God brought the animals to Noah, so God brought talented, dedicated people to AiG to be a part of this cutting edge ministry."

Stephanie McDorman

Perry McDorman

Dan Carlson

Jon Taylor

James de Leon and Kristen Andersen

Sharon Mardis and Amy Stauffer provided valuable assistance to the teams that designed and built the museum.

When Mike hired Patrick Marsh in 2001, the design for the shape and size of the museum had already been approved. This required him to be even more creative in his exhibit design and to try unusual things to fit in the available space.

Patrick Marsh and Mike Zovath   **Jon Seest**   **Carolyn Cancelliere and Stephanie Fazekas**   **Jesse Pié and Travis Wilson**   **Cathy and Doug Henderson**   **Mark Coe**

The design team created concept sketches and then transformed them into scale models of the exhibits, which the fabricators used to build the actual exhibits.

FABRICATION

Although AiG outsourced some of the exhibits, the work of the in-house artists and fabricators can be seen throughout the museum. Their work continues through the present as they continually add new items and exhibits to the museum, making it an ever-"evolving" place.

In 2004 the building was complete. The next concern was how to get the specialty exhibit construction completed while Patrick continued to design details. God then brought LeRoy LaMontagne to AiG. LeRoy owned a custom architectural woodworking business in Knoxville, Tennessee. But when he

heard of AiG's need for help, he packed up all his tools and machines, closed his 22-year-old business, and moved his family to Petersburg, Kentucky.

LeRoy coordinated the specialty contractors, as well as the normal exhibit fabrication and construction (shop and equipment needs, plumbing, code issues, permits, fire suppression, specialty lighting, and electrical). Our fabricators were able to build many of the exhibit areas themselves. Their work continues today as they update exhibits and manufacture new ones.

Mark Hetzel   Gary Lay   Bob Kessler   LeRoy LaMontagne

Adam Partlow   Gary Moon   Kim Hoffman   Allen Jefferies

The fabrication team used the sketches and models created by the design team to build the actual exhibits.

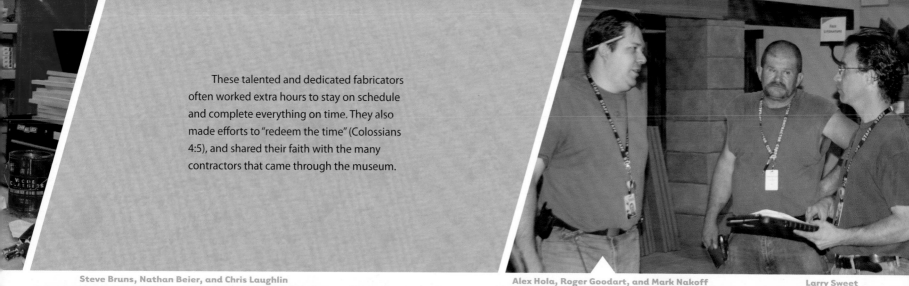

These talented and dedicated fabricators often worked extra hours to stay on schedule and complete everything on time. They also made efforts to "redeem the time" (Colossians 4:5), and shared their faith with the many contractors that came through the museum.

Steve Bruns, Nathan Beier, and Chris Laughlin

Alex Hola, Roger Goodart, and Mark Nakoff

Larry Sweet

Dave Wolfer

Ethan McKeever

Denver Seely

Chuck Steinmetz and Mark WIlkins

CONTENT

While Patrick Marsh oversaw the exhibit design, and LeRoy LaMontagne oversaw the exhibit fabrication, Michael Matthews oversaw the exhibit content. It was Mike's job to make sure his team was compiling the most up-to-date scientific and theological information for each exhibit.

Many PhD scientists and experts were consulted as content was being developed. These included Kurt Wise (the primary consultant), Joe Taylor (dig site), Andrew Snelling (Flood geology), Mike Oard (Ice Age), Tim Lovett (Noah's Ark), Emil Silvestru (caves), Jason Lisle (astronomy), John Baumgardner (plate tectonics), and many others including AiG staff members David Menton and Terry Mortenson.

The Content Team worked for over two years with hundreds of meetings, proposals, and concepts to finalize the content for each of the signs, rooms, video scripts, and teaching points throughout the museum.

Drs. Marcus Ross and Kurt Wise, museum consultants

Mike Matthews (*standing*) leads the Content Team in discussion.

Buddy Davis had been sculpting dinosaurs for years. They were his passion, and his bread-and-butter. He and his wife Kay toured the country with their dinosaurs, showing them in malls and other places. But he wasn't allowed to share the true Bible-based history of dinosaurs. He yearned to use his dinosaurs to tell people the truth.

And then he met Ken Ham. In 1994, at a seminar in Mt. Vernon, Ohio, Buddy invited Ken, Mike, and Mark to his cabin nearby, offering to show them his dinosaurs. These men immediately saw the potential excitement Buddy's dinosaurs could add to the museum, and a friendship was born. Over ten years later, Buddy's dinosaurs began finding homes throughout the Creation Museum. Many currently reside in the special Dinosaur Den.

When Ken first visited Buddy after the seminar, he noticed a guitar in the corner of the room and asked Buddy to play a song. Buddy sang "He Makes Dreams out of Nothing." Ken determined then and there that Buddy should sing that song at the opening of the Creation Museum, which Buddy did in May 2007.

T-rex under construction

Buddy Davis

More than 20 of Buddy's life-size dinosaur models are spread throughout the museum.

Even with the commitment to making the Creation Museum an experiential place, no "natural" history museum is complete without showcasing fossils and other relics. Some of the Creation Museum's collection can stand with the best of museums. The Lord brought along many individuals who donated rare and unusual specimens, including fossils like this unique fish-eating-a-fish fossil.

SEVEN C's

Ken Ham has used the Seven C's of History as a teaching point in his talks for many years. A great device to easily remember the history of the world as presented by the Bible, the Seven C's became the backbone for the museum storyline. Cartoonist Dan Lietha created the original illustrations, which became well known from their use in multiple presentations, books, and videos. Jon Seest's redesign brings a contemporary look, suitable for the museum.

BEFORE

AFTER

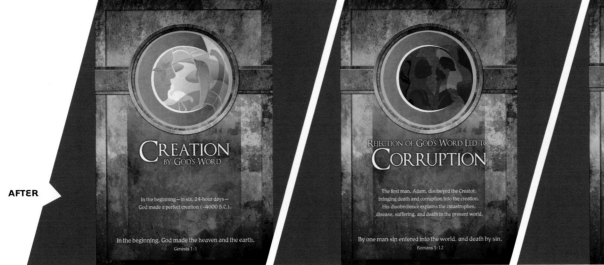 

CREATION
BY GOD'S WORD

In the beginning—in six, 24-hour days—
God made a perfect creation (~4000 B.C.).

In the beginning, God made the heaven and the earth.
Genesis 1:1

REJECTION OF GOD'S WORD LED TO
CORRUPTION

The first man, Adam, disobeyed the Creator,
bringing death and corruption into the creation.
His disobedience explains the catastrophes,
disease, suffering, and death in the present world.

By one man sin entered into the world, and death by sin.
Romans 5:12

REJECTION OF GOD'S WORD LED TO
CATASTROPHE

Adam's race became so wicked that God judged
the earth with a catastrophic, global Flood, saving
only those on the Ark built by Noah (~2348 B.C.).
This global catastrophe resulted in fossils
all over the earth.

God said, "I do bring a flood of
waters upon the earth, to destroy all flesh."
Genesis 6:17

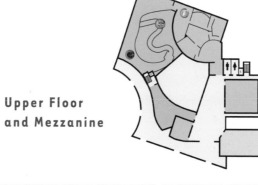

Upper Floor and Mezzanine

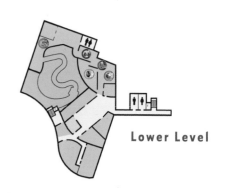

Lower Level

REJECTION OF GOD'S WORD LED TO
CONFUSION

When Noah's descendants disobeyed God's command to fill the earth, God gave them different languages, forcing them to spread over the earth. The scattering of people explains the formation of different people groups.

The Lord did confound the language of all the earth and...scatter them abroad.
Genesis 11:9

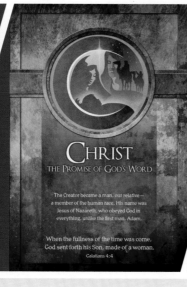

CHRIST
THE PROMISE OF GOD'S WORD

The Creator became a man, our relative — a member of the human race. His name was Jesus of Nazareth, who obeyed God in everything, unlike the first man, Adam.

When the fullness of the time was come, God sent forth his Son, made of a woman.
Galatians 4:4

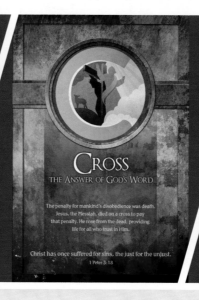

CROSS
THE ANSWER OF GOD'S WORD

The penalty for mankind's disobedience was death. Jesus, the Messiah, died on a cross to pay that penalty. He rose from the dead, providing life for all who trust in Him.

Christ has once suffered for sins, the just for the unjust.
1 Peter 3:18

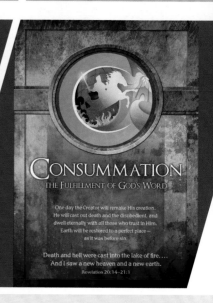

CONSUMMATION
THE FULFILLMENT OF GOD'S WORD

One day the Creator will remake His creation. He will cast out death and the disobedient, and dwell eternally with all those who trust in Him. Earth will be restored to a perfect place — as it was before sin.

Death and hell were cast into the lake of fire.... And I saw a new heaven and a new earth.
Revelation 20:14–21:1

BTS TOURS

Charter memberships turned out to be a great source of support. With the membership package, members were given the opportunity to attend several Behind the Scenes (BTS) tours during the construction of the museum where they were able to see the museum at various stages of its progress.

The entire museum team demonstrated their various contributions to the project and interacted with the members. The tours were stopped after April of 2006 when the AiG board mandated an opening date of May 2007. The huge push to finish the museum would not allow the interruption to the schedules of contractors that the tours required.

By the end of the offered tours, the crowds had grown to such a large number that museum planners began to reevaluate the expected crowd sizes for the finished museum. This reevaluation led to the decision to enclose the portico to provide additional indoor lobby space, expand the café space, and change some of the exhibit plans to provide better flow through the museum.

Early Behind the Scenes tour groups saw the museum in a very bare-bones state. Museum artists set up wall panels and wire mannequins to give guests an idea what the rooms would contain and painted arrows on the floor to direct guests through the still non-existent walk-through.

Some of the Behind the Scenes tours provided the children of charter members with personal interaction with Buddy Davis and Ken Ham.

Members were given photo opportunities with Ken Ham and Buddy Davis.

The large BTS crowds gave Mike Zovath and his operations team a preview of the possible numbers that the museum might see when it opened, leading to changes in certain areas (such as the portico, Noah's Café, and the Six Days Theater) to help accommodate such crowds.

RIBBON CUTTING

Occupancy was granted only hours before the museum opened for a preview week for museum members. The scheduled ribbon cutting brought in a large crowd of by-invitation-only guests and media. Notable guests included Boone County Judge Executive Gary W. Moore, Boone County Commissioner Charles Kenner, Boone County Circuit Judge Linda Bramlage, Kentucky Commerce Cabinet Secretary George Ward, Kentucky State Senators Dick Roeding and Jack Westwood, Kentucky State Representatives Addia Wuchner and Tom Kerr, and Kentucky Court of Appeals Judge Joy Moore. Over 130 separate media organizations requested press credentials for the week.

Final occupancy granted just in time! 5-19-07

Ken Ham, Mark Looy, Patrick Marsh, Mike Zovath, and Don Landis (Chairman of the AiG Board) prepare to cut the ribbon, opening the Creation Museum on May 26, 2007.

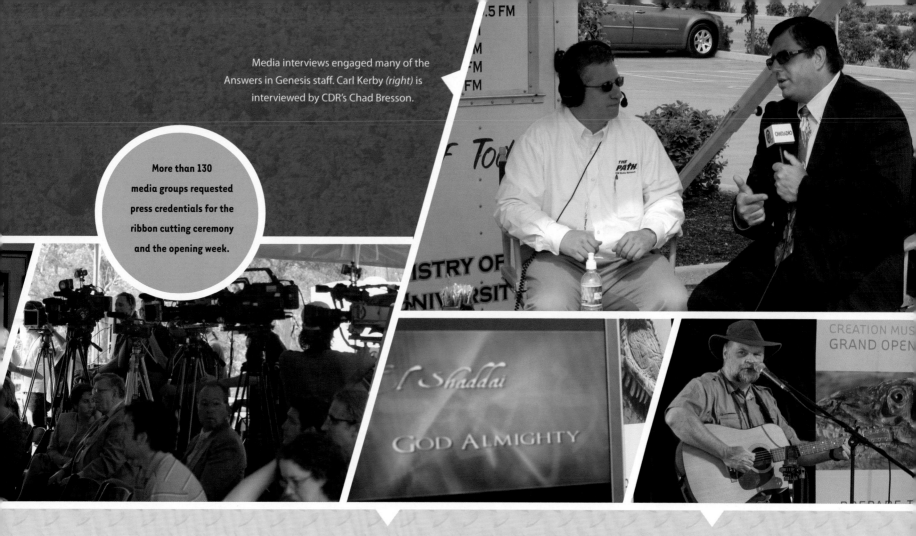

Media interviews engaged many of the Answers in Genesis staff. Carl Kerby *(right)* is interviewed by CDR's Chad Bresson.

More than 130 media groups requested press credentials for the ribbon cutting ceremony and the opening week.

In the ceremony, Ken showed a moving video on the names of God and gave God all the glory for the building of this museum.

Buddy sang his song "He Makes Dreams out of Nothing."

GRAND OPENING

Months before the scheduled grand opening, an anti-creation group called Rally for Reason put out an invitation on the Internet for protestors to rally outside the Creation Museum on opening day. The crowd of protestors was not as large as anticipated, but it provided an entertaining gauntlet for the 4,000 guests who came to the opening to show their support.

A group called DefCon rented a plane to fly an anti-museum banner (below) around the property for the entire weekend. Unfortunately for them, many of the guests of the museum did not understand the point they were attempting to make and mistook the banner as an advertisement for the museum!

A few dozen protestors lined the approach to the museum on opening day.

Footage of the protestors on opening day appeared in Ben Stein's feature documentary, *Expelled: No Intelligence Allowed.*

The lines inside the museum were long . . .

The media were everywhere.

A patient and supportive crowd put up with long lines and constant media attention to be counted as our supporters on Grand Opening Day. Nearly 4,000 people toured the museum. Thankfully, clouds kept the temperature bearable.

. . . the lines outside the museum were longer.

Ken fielded countless interviews.

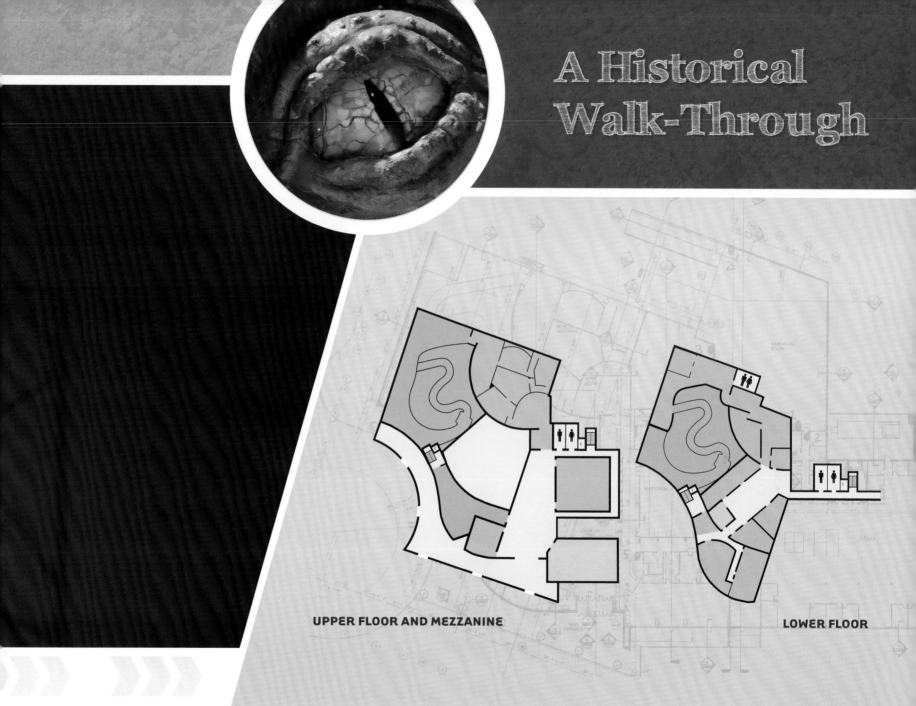

A Historical Walk-Through

UPPER FLOOR AND MEZZANINE

LOWER FLOOR

PORTICO

MAIN GATE & PORTICO

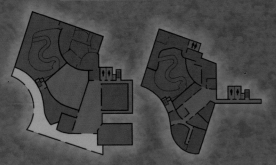

The original plan for the strata-like portico wall was to have an actual cast of a section of Grand Canyon with embedded dinosaur fossils. After receiving permission to make this cast from a tribal council that controls that piece of land, a single tribal official reversed the decision. Instead, the wall is a cast from layers in an outcrop in northern Connecticut. It is still quite stunning.

Public polls that we commissioned, comments from local media and officials, and the incredible response to memberships showed us that the originally designed lobby would be woefully inadequate to handle the expected crowds. So a decision was made to enclose the portico in glass. This required engineering designs, county approval, permits, air conditioning and heating, etc.

The decision to have dinosaurs at the main gate came early.

The portico's molded wall, which came in huge sheets of fiberglass, was assembled like a giant jigsaw puzzle.

The original pavers used for the exterior patio were kept as the floor of the new indoor portico.

6,800 square feet were added to the museum by enclosing the exterior portico.

MAIN HALL

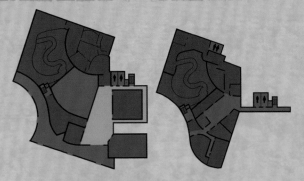

The Main Hall (originally referred to as the Lobby) remained largely consistent from concept to development. The only major difference between the original concept and its final appearance was the location of the animatronic children and dinosaurs. The Main Hall was originally conceived as the lobby inside the main double entry of the museum. Later examination of this plan proved the area too small to handle ticket sales and other lines. The then-exterior frontage of the museum seemed a more logical place for ticket sales and also for information and member desks. It was too open to inclement weather, though, so the entire area was enclosed in glass, and the double entrance in front of the Main Hall was removed to provide open access. The Main Hall is now the staging area for Noah's Café, the Men in White Special Effects Theater, the Stargazers Planetarium, and Dragon Hall Bookstore, as well as the entrance to the museum walk-through.

Incorporating a large water feature inside a building not originally designed for it was quite a challenge.

The rocks in the Main Hall (and throughout the museum) started out as large foam blocks.

One of the purposes for the pond was to feature "living fossils," animals which are in the fossil record and have not changed for evolution's assumed "millions of years," such as the gar fish, turtles, and the nearby Bald Cypress trees.

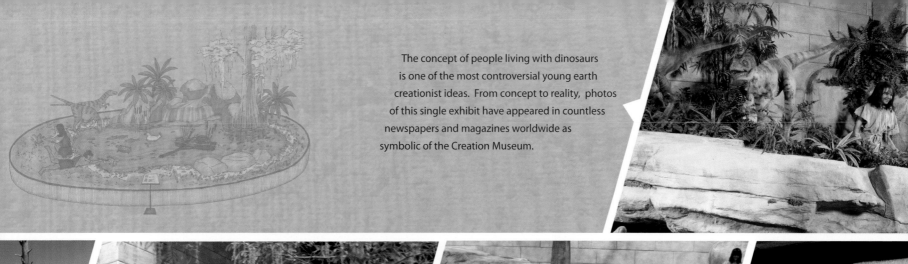

The concept of people living with dinosaurs is one of the most controversial young earth creationist ideas. From concept to reality, photos of this single exhibit have appeared in countless newspapers and magazines worldwide as symbolic of the Creation Museum.

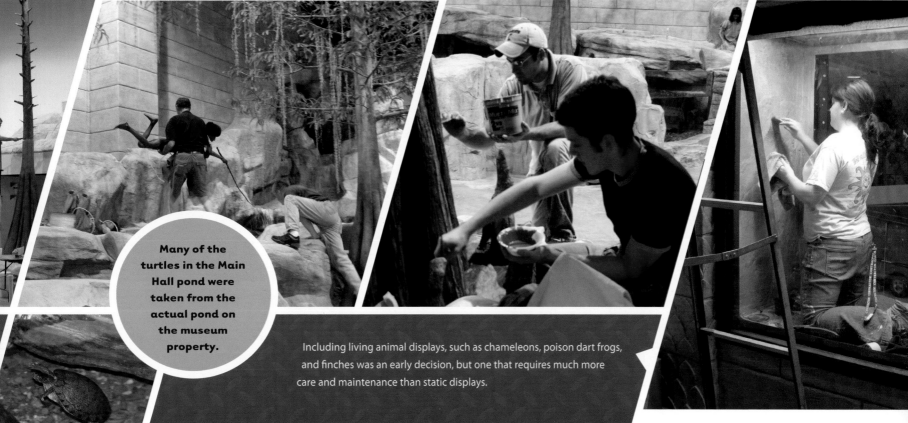

Many of the turtles in the Main Hall pond were taken from the actual pond on the museum property.

Including living animal displays, such as chameleons, poison dart frogs, and finches was an early decision, but one that requires much more care and maintenance than static displays.

NOAH'S CAFÉ

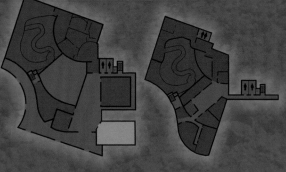

Original concepts for the museum did not include a café. Concerns over food service regulations and the cost involved made the whole idea bigger than planners wanted to deal with. Though space was set aside in the original plans for food service, that space was labeled as a vending machine area, though there was some thought of bringing in a third-party vendor.

Plans changed when supporters Darryl and Deb Cordrey, full-time food service managers, stepped forward and offered their expertise in establishing and operating a full-service café. Noah's Café was born out of that arrangement and opened for staff and construction workers in 2006. The bare-bones cafe offered sandwiches and wraps and a daily hot entrée until it was closed for the final expansion and construction.

Darryl Cordrey

Deb Cordrey

The café floor was stamped to achieve a fossil-look—representing the aftermath of Noah's Flood.

The original café plan included an open feeling, with portable cooking units on wheels that could be moved around. Once we realized the numbers of people that would be coming through, the units were permanently installed.

The café was outgrown long before it opened to the public, and museum planners doubled the seating to well over 300 by enclosing the original patio and adding much larger decks. The expansion vision also required additional food service in the Palm Plaza and outside next to the lake. Both of these were added after the museum opened as funds became available.

Noah's Café contains one of the many fabulous murals that can be seen throughout the museum.

STARGAZERS PLANETARIUM

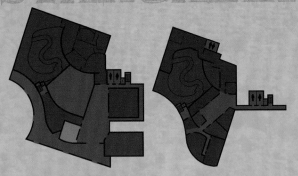

The Stargazers Planetarium wasn't even a part of the plans until an antique planetarium projector, which had once been used to train NASA's Mercury astronauts, was donated to the museum by Mr. John Dilday. Space was then carved out of the bookstore to build a theater for the refurbished planetarium projector.

By the time the project was complete, astrophysicist Dr. Jason Lisle, designer and programmer of the now–popular planetarium shows, had convinced the museum management that a more state-of-the-art projector was needed. As a result, the Stargazers Planetarium is now a versatile addition to the Creation Museum, able to run many different programs depending on season and emphasis, as well as accommodate live lectures. The NASA projector is a piece of American history, on permanent display in the portico.

John Dilday

The Digistar 3 SP2 digital projection system replaced the old planetarium projector and now provides guests with a breathtaking view of the cosmos. We were one of the first planetariums to begin using this new technology.

The projection dome was purchased used and then refurbished prior to installation.

The hand-woven carpet in the planetarium was created in Germany specially for the Creation Museum and donated by a businessman in Northern Ireland.

Reclining planetarium seats were purchased and shipped from Spain.

The program shown when the museum opened, "The Created Cosmos," was actually the second one that Dr. Jason Lisle (left) created. The first was "Worlds of Creation."

SPECIAL EFFECTS THEATER

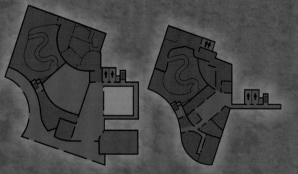

One of the first rooms to be used as the museum interior progressed was the large 200-seat Special Effects Theater. Seats were installed just in time as Answers in Genesis staff outgrew the room where regular staff meetings were held. Since this time, the staff has met in this theater twice a week for ministry-wide devotions and was the first to experience the special effects of the *Men in White* movie well before the museum opened.

AiG staff began using the theater for meetings as soon as seats were installed.

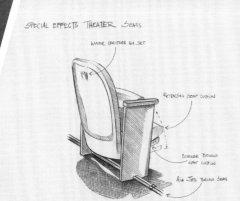

SPECIAL EFFECTS THEATER SEATS

WATER CONTROL AIR JET

RETAINING SEAT CUSHION

BUBBLER BELOW SEAT CUSHION

AIR JETS BELOW SEATS

The original chairs were replaced with new high-tech seating because it was determined that it would be more expensive to retrofit them with water and vibration than it would be to purchase new ones already outfitted with these features. But there was no waste of chairs. All of the original seats were installed in the two new theaters established for the Last Adam and Dragon Legends movies.

Wendy, the animatronic star of the show, is often mistaken for a real girl!

What's this? Water pipes in a theater?

Wendy has questions. They have answers.

MEN IN WHITE

Grooters Productions in association with Answers In Genesis presents "Men In White" starring John Alsopp and Michael Downing story by John Grooters executive producer Patrick Marsh and Mike Zovath music by Eric Schrotenboer director of photography Max Penner executive producer Eric Schrotenboer directed by John Grooters

Mike and Gabe (the angels in *Men in White*) were shot in a Hollywood studio in front of a 60-foot tall greenscreen used for flying scenes in movies such as *Superman*.

AiG staff and contractors gather to see the new SFX presentation.

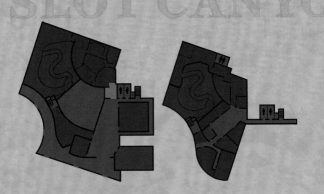

The purpose of the slot canyon is to raise questions that will be answered later in the museum experience. This includes the provocative question asked as one enters: "Ever wonder where canyons come from?"

Painting the canyon walls was difficult since the canyon is the only entrance into the walk-through from the top floor, so the painters (such as Ron Hight above) worked late into the night to be able to paint uninterrupted.

Both photos (Grand Canyon and Mount St. Helens) were taken specifically for this display in the museum and donated by the photographer.

DIG SITE

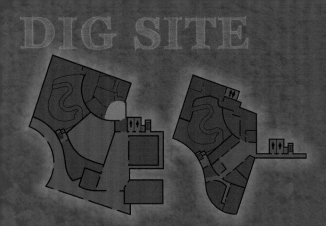

A dinosaur dig site in the middle of a museum? How does that happen? With a lot of preplanning and work.

Original artist concept

The Utahraptor fossil was sculpted by Buddy Davis for this exhibit. Another copy was made and shipped to Utah to make the video that is now seen in this room. After the video shoot was completed, it was shipped back to the museum, where it is now in storage.

Dirtying up the floor on purpose—workers glue sand to the concrete to create a "natural" floor for the dig site.

Paleontologist Joe Taylor helped in the design and installation of the dig site. His experience in the real world of paleontology was crucial in designing an authentic-looking site.

The rock-like walls were fabricated off-site and put up in a matter of days.

There are hidden windows in the dig site room which overlook the fabrication room. Original concepts allowed guests to look down on the inner workings of the museum.

STARTING POINTS

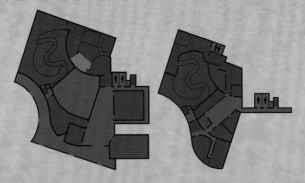

This room is crucial to setting the stage for the rest of the museum experience. And this room was the hardest to finalize—concepts and designs kept changing from month to month.

One of the challenges in this room was to demonstrate the differences between God's Word and man's fallible ideas without looking neutral. At the same time, we did not want to be seen as attacking the evolutionists and their beliefs.

The animatronic Utahraptor that is now part of Corruption Valley was originally in the Starting Points room. However, it was decided that the raptor was too distracting and diverted attention away from the important teaching points, so he was moved.

The children pointing the way to the Biblical Authority room were modeled after children of museum employees.

The sculpted raptor was built on-site by the museum design team.

BIBLICAL AUTHORITY

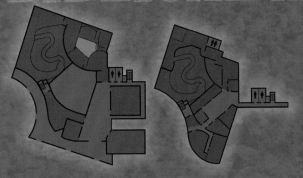

In this room, we wanted to set the stage for the Creation Walk, by showing guests that the Bible can be trusted and that it gives us a reliable account of history. This room combines many different materials and textures, and elements that were built by both in-house staff and outside contractors.

The characters in the room (and throughout the museum) were created by an outside company that also built the figures of Lincoln for the Lincoln Museum in Illinois. Originally we were going to use clay sculptures, but we decided we wanted the more life-like approach that could be achieved with silicone casts.

After choosing LifeFormations to create the figures in the museum, we discovered that the head art designer assigned to our project was a creationist—a rarity in this industry. She approached her job with great passion and attention to detail, and considered it to be a ministry.

The replica of the Gutenberg Press was donated to the museum.

CULTURE IN CRISIS

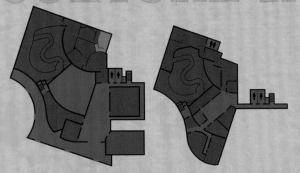

This room is basically a queue for the Six Days Theater. The purpose of this room is to make guests think while they are waiting and to experience a bit of the effects of compromise in our churches. Adirondack Scenic was the vendor who fabricated this area based on Patrick Marsh's designs. They are a professional design firm which has done work in theaters, arenas, exhibit halls, ballrooms, parks, restaurants, malls, supermarkets, museums, stadiums, main streets, and marinas.

The newspaper and magazine clippings were collected from hundreds of sources that spanned a seven-year period. This is a "living wall," with the ability to add more articles and headlines as they appear in the press.

The theme of this room was inspired by the "two castles" diagram often used by Ken Ham to show the world's attack on the foundation of Christianity—the book of Genesis.

The elements of this room were built off-site and the whole area was assembled in three days inside the museum.

This room was intended to be dark and reveal man's sinfulness, creating a contrast with God's "very good" creation shown in the Six Days Theater (the next room).

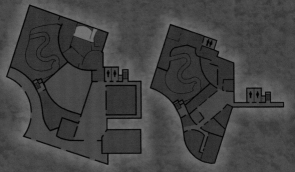

This room represents a major transition in the museum—going back in time 6,000 years to the creation of the world. We decided to let Scripture speak for itself, and so we just used the text of Genesis 1 for the presentation.

The original concept for the Time Tunnel was similar to the one on the *Time Tunnel* science fiction TV series of the late 1960s—a spinning tunnel through which people would walk. This idea was dropped due to practical design considerations and the fear that it may make people dizzy.

Some of the artwork featured in the Six Days movie was created "on the fly" by our art director Jon Taylor while at Grooters production studio in Michigan, during post-production.

This area was used for months as a tree manufacturing room where all of the trees for the Creation Walk were built.

The original design for the Six Days Theater was three rooms, each depicting two days of creation. It was decided to combine them into one larger theater, with a very wide screen to show the four-minute video of Genesis 1.

SIX DAYS
THEATER

SPECIAL WONDERS

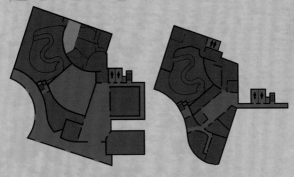

The original concept for the Special Wonders room was much different than what was actually built. The original concept called for individual stations with interactive ways to learn the various bits of creation information from DNA to animal kinds.

The concept then changed to a larger open floor plan with various videos playing simultaneously throughout the room. However, after the museum had been open for several weeks, we changed it so that all the monitors now play through the same loop of 15 informative videos. Much of the scientific content of the museum is presented in these videos.

This room is a great place to sit down and rest, while learning snippets of interesting information on a variety of topics on the wonders of creation.

The design of this room intentionally integrated smooth lines rather than hard edges to feel more organic—more like God's work than man's.

The overhead sails need to be taken down twice each year to be treated with fire retardant. A small section of the fabric is then cut from the sail and tested to recertify that is is fireproof.

Fifteen high-quality science videos play on continuous loop.

This area was used as a sculpting studio for months while animals were created for the Creation Walk.

So that men are *Without* Exc...

CREATION WALK

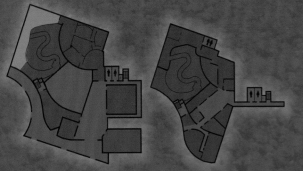

The Main Floor and Creation Walk ramp were built long before the space was properly planned. Therefore, the concepts underwent a great many changes before final exhibit construction actually began.

Animatronic Utahraptor

First Sacrifice

Cave of Sorrows

Adam and Eve in the pool

Corruption Valley

Cain kills Abel

The Creation Walk's descent mirrors mankind's descent from the Garden of Eden.

Many guests don't realize they are descending gradually as they walk down the Creation Walk. In this picture, you can get an idea of the actual progression of the walk without the exhibits to hide the descent. This descent mirrors mankind's descent from the Garden of Eden to God's judgment at the Flood.

A 3D model of a portion of the Creation Walk

The early plans for the Creation Walk featured Buddy Davis's life-size *T. rex* model, which had been completed before the museum building was finished and stored at AiG's rented warehouse space in Florence, Kentucky. Before the final doorways could be hung on the main floor of the museum, the temporarily headless *T. rex* was shipped by truck to the museum and assembled next to the Creation Walk ramp, where he awed behind-the-scenes visitors for a couple years. Later, plans for the space required his removal. However, he would not fit through the doors, and so he was disassembled and installed in his present location on the second floor of the Dinosaur Den.

Creation of Eve

Adam names the animals

Noah's Ark dioramas

Flood Geology

The original concept included live alligators!

CREATED KINDS

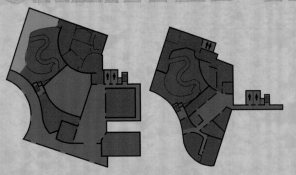

One of the greatest challenges that the content and artistic teams faced was how to portray the original animal kinds of Genesis 1. Coming up with how each of the animals might have looked in the Garden of Eden was an ongoing and highly difficult task that required hours of exhaustive research and many trials with miniature models.

Also, every plant and prop in the museum had to be fire retarded. Each item had to be individually tested to determine which fire retardant product would work. Hundreds of failed tests were conducted before we found the correct combination that would allow each item to pass. Testing of every item took over six weeks. After the testing was done, production lines were set up over a course of three months with more than 100 volunteers who helped to treat every plant and most products before they were installed.

Ninety percent of the animal sculptures started with taxidermy forms which were shaped by adding epoxy and then carved, textured, and painted to make the final animal.

It was eventually decided to exclude the giraffe from the animal exhibit based on its absence from the fossil record of the Flood as well as our model of created kinds and rapid speciation after the Flood.

Sculptors put thousands of hours into researching and sculpting the animals.

Our artists often placed the animals while still in the process of construction so they could see how they fit in their environment.

CREATION WALK

THE GARDEN & THE TREES

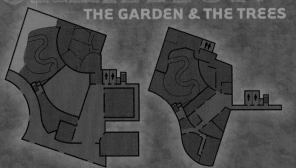

The rocks and structures on the Creation Walk were built out of fireproof wood and steel, then clad with white foam blocks, each the size of a refrigerator! The foam was shaped by hand using hot wires and knives, saws, and wire brushes. The surface of the foam was often covered with wire mesh before liquid cement was sprayed over it.

The cement was applied in two layers. The first was sprayed on then spread with a serrated trowel to give it a texture that the next layer would bond well to. The second layer was worked by hand with trowels, brushes, and various sculpting tools to get the textures to look real. Finally, all of the concrete surfaces were sealed and painted with house paint.

The branches for the Tree of Life were made from muffler pipe wrapped with foam.

Every piece of foliage was installed into hand-drilled holes, or special bases were created and mounted and then the trees and plants were attached to those.

Every detail in the museum was compared to the biblical account. As an example, the Tree of Life bears 12 fruits and 12 flowers for the next month's fruit, as is mentioned in Revelation 22:2.

With so many people working in and around various ongoing projects, signs began popping up all over the museum expressing certain heart-felt warnings on behalf of the artists at work!

If you are not an expert mural painter able to repaint this wall! Do not put anything on it including your hands!

The scaffolding was reused for handrails both inside and outside the museum

The construction of the Tree of Life reminded the workers of the tree house in the film *The Swiss Family Robinson*. It was by far the largest construction project inside the museum. It is 25 feet tall, sticks out from the wall 35 feet, and is 50 feet wide at its widest. 31,104 leaves cover its branches.

CORRUPTION

So what did the serpent in the Garden of Eden look like? No one today knows, so it takes an artist's vision to bring this ultimate villain to life. Creation Museum artists were challenged to each come up with a concept for the serpent in or near the tree.

The Tree of the Knowledge of Good and Evil is about the size of just one of the branches of the Tree of Life. The idea was to emphasize the abundance of God's provision for life and the fact that Adam and Eve had everything they needed. They weren't eating from the Tree of Knowledge because they had nothing else to eat—they were eating out of rebellion against their Creator.

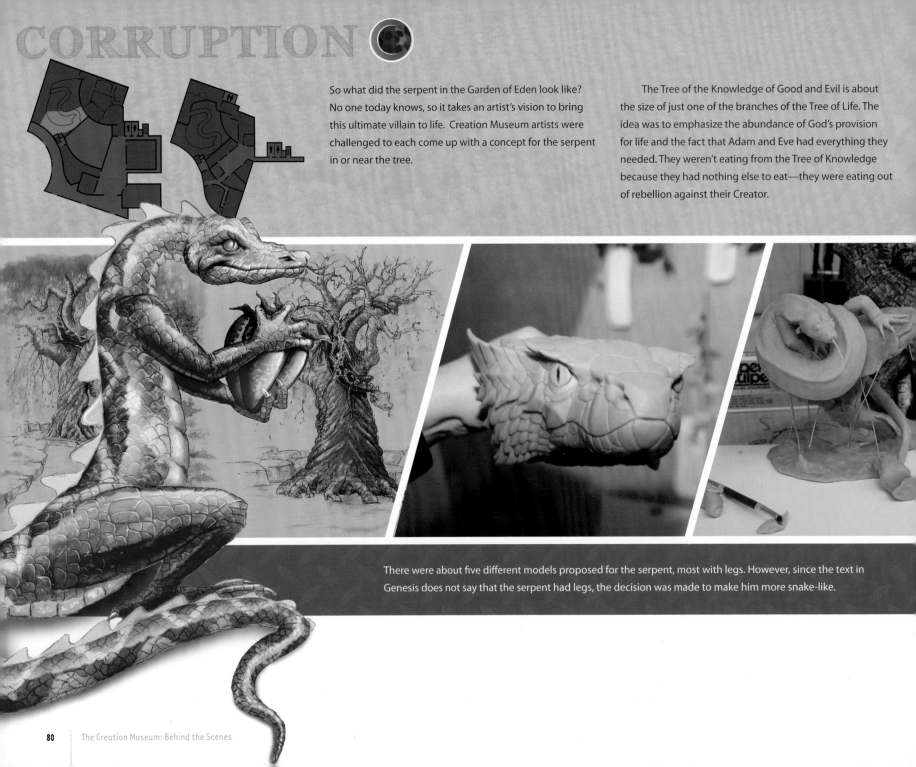

There were about five different models proposed for the serpent, most with legs. However, since the text in Genesis does not say that the serpent had legs, the decision was made to make him more snake-like.

Grapes were chosen to represent the fruit that Eve ate and gave to Adam because according to some ancient Jewish teachings the forbidden fruit was the grape from which wine is derived.

The scales on the serpent are actually pumpkin seeds glued on one at a time and sealed with fiberglass resin.

The serpent in the tree near Adam and Eve was not painted until the night before the museum's grand opening. Many of these last-minute details were addressed in one long, last-ditch effort by the majority of the museum's creative team, who put in very long hours during the months leading up to the museum's scheduled opening.

CORRUPTION

CORRUPTION VALLEY

Corruption Valley was designed to showcase the horrible effects of the Fall, including carnivory, death, disease, pain in childbirth, etc. Designers wanted to make it dark and shocking, while at the same time taking into account that children would be viewing. Much thought went into how much blood to show and how graphic the images should be.

Mike Zovath first saw the animatronic Utahraptor (above, left) at a convention and knew we had to have it, but Advanced Animations, its creator, had it listed for $75,000 and would not come down on the price. It was subsequently sold, but the purchaser backed out, so after four months of it sitting in their warehouse, they agreed to sell it to the Creation Museum for only $33,000.

The shape and design of Adam's house demonstrates advanced construction techniques, similar to those used in some stone houses today. We wanted to show that Adam was an intelligent, creative man.

Even the museum figures participated in the final clean up!

Adam's house was one of the first structures to appear on the Creation Walk once the exhibit design started in earnest. It took many months for surrounding structures to fill in around it. The rocks are hand sculpted out of foam as are most of the rocks throughout the museum.

CATASTROPHE

NOAH'S ARK & THE GREAT FLOOD

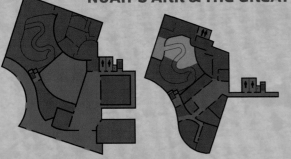

How do you fit a 510-foot boat inside a small space? You don't. You show a segment of it. Just a small portion of Noah's Ark (about 1%) is sufficient to give guests a feel of the true scale of this massive ship. Proceeding down into the Flood exhibit space, small dioramas show the progression of the Flood as well as the solutions to how animals were kept and cared for within the Ark.

It was a big decision to move away from the box-like Ark shape that has endured for decades to a curved ship-like design, but still adhering to the Bible's dimensions. The new design has been warmly received given the adherence to the Bible's measurements and Tim Lovett's extensive research behind the new design.

Noah was eventually positioned by this "cubit table," a work bench with cubit measurements and tools that Noah might have used. This table took months to build by master woodworker Gene Earnest and demonstrates the attention to detail and quality taken in the exhibit construction.

How did Noah care for all the animals? Dioramas showing how animals could have been housed and cared for was a priority in the Noah's Ark exhibit.

Tim Lovett (left) was hired in early 2006. His vast research on the Ark caused a total redesign of this area, and much more room was given to the exhibit than originally planned.

FLOOD GEOLOGY

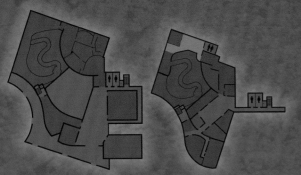

In this area we wanted to show that real science supports the Bible, and when it comes to mechanisms for the Flood, much research has been done by creation scientists. This space was expanded from its original design as the content team consulted with scientists and determined that there was much to say on this topic. The design includes videos, dioramas, signs, and models to engage the senses and demonstrate that the Bible can be trusted.

The large mural in the Flood Geology room depicts over 40 creatures from the fossil record. It was designed to counter the Yale Peabody Museum's "Age of Reptiles" mural. Our mural shows these creatures over space rather than over time.

Mark Coe was the muralist who created all the wonderful murals in the Creation Museum. He had been painting murals as well as designing, fabricating, and installing natural history museum exhibits for about 15 years before joining our project.

Geologist Dr. Andrew Snelling consults with Mike Matthews on the science in the Flood Geology room.

Planned from the beginning, and once hidden behind a wall in the Flood Geology exhibit area, a cave exhibit, which was to feature an experiment growing stalactites and stalagmites, ran into feasibility issues which sadly kept it from ever seeing the light of day. The space now houses an exhibit on natural selection.

CONFUSION

BABEL

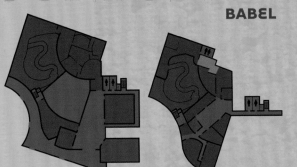

Like many spaces in the museum, the concept for the Babel exhibit went through many modifications from paper to completion. Changes were due to feasibility, cost, and time concerns. This area highlights the work of many sculptors, painters, carpenters, and masons.

The original idea was to project the Tower of Babel movie onto a waterfall "screen." Feasibility issues and cost concerns changed this plan.

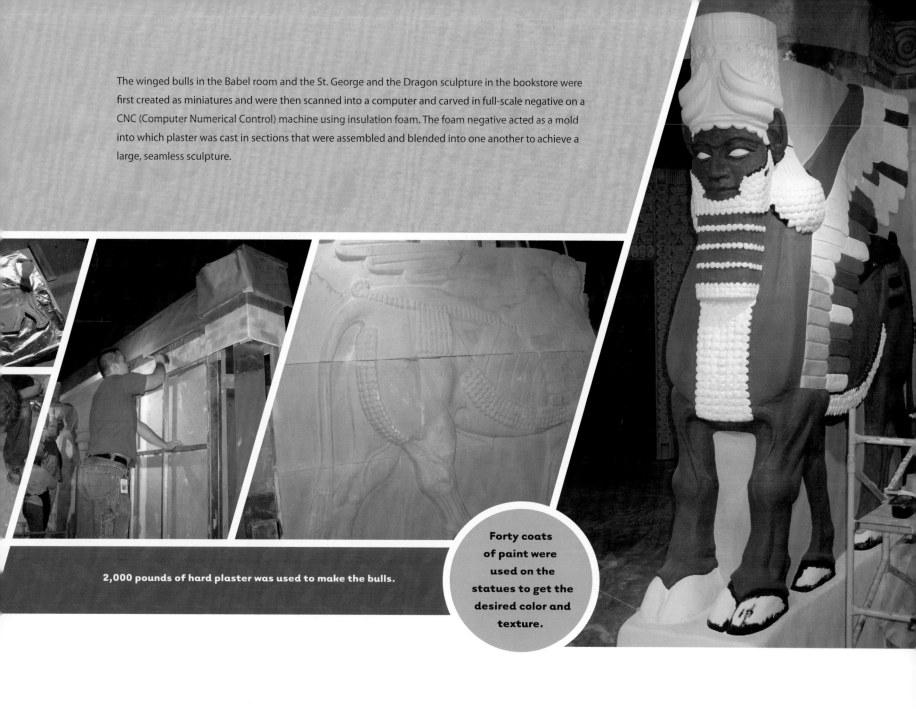

The winged bulls in the Babel room and the St. George and the Dragon sculpture in the bookstore were first created as miniatures and were then scanned into a computer and carved in full-scale negative on a CNC (Computer Numerical Control) machine using insulation foam. The foam negative acted as a mold into which plaster was cast in sections that were assembled and blended into one another to achieve a large, seamless sculpture.

2,000 pounds of hard plaster was used to make the bulls.

Forty coats of paint were used on the statues to get the desired color and texture.

LAST ADAM

The original concept for the last three C's of history was animatronic characters telling their stories to guests who would gather around them. This idea was eventually discarded and replaced with a high-impact movie entitled *The Last Adam*, which incorporates the idea in the form of live actors playing the parts of Mary the mother of Jesus and the centurion who crucified Jesus.

This is one of four theaters in the Creation Museum, in addition to the planetarium.

Switching to a movie required a theater and a waiting area to queue guests for each showing. The seats were scavenged from the Special Effects Theater when new seats were installed there. AiG staff members served as test audiences to help work out capacities and flow. The movie is back projected using three digital projectors.

The Last Adam movie was shot at the Holy Land Experience park in Orlando, Florida at a cost of about $150,000.

THE LAST ADAM

PALM PLAZA

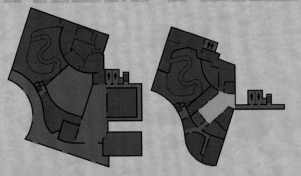

Originally conceived as an area for rotating exhibits, the Palm Plaza is now a place for rest, reflection, and refreshment.

There are over 1,100 hand-textured, painted, and glazed boards that make up the stone wall of the Palm Plaza.

About 140 gallons of thinset (light-weight cement) were used in the Palm Plaza.

A simple refreshment bar was expanded into a burrito bar restaurant to relieve some of the crowding in Noah's Café upstairs.

Coins tossed into the Palm Plaza fountain go toward maintenance and repair of equipment.

The original waterfall design had to be altered to a flat wall fountain because of the need for office space behind the fountain.

DRAGON HALL BOOKSTORE

We wanted the bookstore to be an exhibit itself, not merely a place to purchase books and gifts. Much work went into the design and building of this space, including the hardwood floors, the large chandelier, the stained-glass windows, the coats of arms, the detailed scroll work, the fireplace, and the dragon that overlooks the store. The store is continually "evolving" as we think of new creative ways to engage customers and display products.

The original theme of Bugs & Books was changed to a medieval castle showcasing dinosaurs and dragon legends.

The labor to install and finish the complex parquet wood floor of the bookstore was donated, and the material was purchased at cost.

The St. George and the Dragon sculpture was first sculpted as ¼ scale model in clay, then scanned into the CNC computer, which created a 3D negative mold. Hydracal plaster was poured into the mold and, after curing, was installed in pieces. St. George needed a good bit of detailing and a light marble faux-finish to make it complete.

Recent high school graduate Travis Wilson (right) sculpted St. George and the Dragon.

The book-reading dragon in the bookstore was first sculpted in the computer using Zbrush. Then, designer Jesse Pié cut the digital model up into slices. These slices were cut out of foam on the CNC machine and then laminated together with an adhesive foam. After much cutting, shaping, and sanding, the final thinset texture and paint were applied, and he was moved to his new home in the bookstore.

RUNNING THE EFFECTS

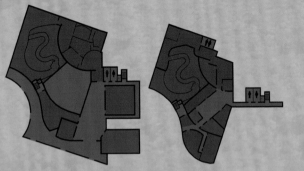

Operating a museum of this scale, with all of the projectors, LCD monitors, animatronics, lighting, and special effects requires an enormous number of computers, servers, and other electronics. Contractors, together with the AiG audio visual team, spent months pulling wire, installing equipment, and testing everything.

AiG houses 29 servers, nine of which are used for museum purposes.

More than 80 miles of A/V cable runs through the museum!

Many of the walls, like the one behind the Special Effects Theater and the wall between the bookstore and planetarium, required special sound-proofing insulation to prevent the films from being heard through the walls.

There are over 17 projectors and 118 speakers throughout the museum.

The museum spends $60,000 annually just to replace projector bulbs!

There are 81 widescreen LCD monitors playing over 50 videos throughout the museum.

GARDENS

Effort went into beautifying not only the exterior and interior of the building, but also the landscape surrounding the Creation Museum. The museum team desired to provide an outdoor space where the Creator's handiwork was admired as such, rather than attributed to naturalistic processes operating blindly over millions of years. The Lord brought along another local resident, horticulturalist Tim Schmitt. Applying their God-given talents, Tim and his team constructed over two miles of trails, with bridges and resting places, which wind their way through a bog, rainforest area, butterfly garden, and petting zoo. Pavilions abound so that guests can enjoy the great outdoors while they have lunch.

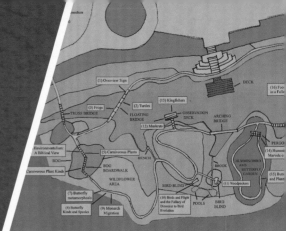

The lake is almost 30 feet deep at its deepest.

Tim Schmitt managed his grounds crew and hundreds of volunteers in transforming a grass field into a beautiful, lush garden area with over 550 varieties of plants.

Gazebo under construction

When the rubber liner for the waterfall was first ordered, the wrong size was shipped. The supplier shipped the right size and told us to keep the first one at no charge, allowing us to extend one of the creeks for free!

There are over two miles of irrigation pipe throughout the gardens.

Over 100,000 bulbs have been planted around the grounds.

The rocks that line the creeks—from the size of a softball to a small car—were hand-picked and placed in position one at a time by our grounds crew.

BRIDGES

Teams of skilled volunteers built the seven different bridges that connect the trails through our botanical gardens. Volunteers from churches came for a week at a time and worked long days to complete these bridges. Without the hard work of all of our volunteers, this museum could not have become a reality. The bridges include a swinging bridge, an arch bridge, a waterfall bridge, a floating bridge, two boardwalks, and a suspension bridge.

The boardwalk was the first bridge completed.

In 2006, Wayne (far right) and Jane Camfield of Greenville, South Carolina, brought more than 20 volunteers who spent three weeks building bridges at the Creation Museum.

The Carnivorous Bog Garden is planted in three feet of peat and sand.

The most popular bridge with kids is the swinging bridge.

A portion of the two-story Dinosaur Den

Only the Beginning

Even in the year following the opening of the museum, things continued to happen. New bathrooms were built, a petting zoo was constructed, the Dinosaur Den opened, and other cafés were added. And the activity won't stop there! Ken explains his vision for the future of the Creation Museum:

> Perhaps the greatest blessing for me would be to see the spiritual legacy of a godly father and mother back in Australia reach hundreds of thousands (and eventually millions) of lives through the museum. That burden, that "fire in my bones," is still being intensified. We can't sit still. What can we do now to reach even more people with the creation/gospel message? I often wonder how we can disseminate even more information and see greater numbers of people. I lie awake at night dreaming and praying about expanding the vision—thinking outside the box. I believe this is just the start—we haven't even scratched the surface. It really is only the beginning.
>
> When one reporter asked me at the opening of the museum, "Do you have any plans for the future, or is this it?" I answered, "You haven't seen anything yet!" If God allows, I believe the Lord has much more in store for this ministry. As Noah's Ark stood as a warning to the world of impending judgment and yet pictured salvation with the door open, so I believe God is using this ministry as He did with Noah: to warn the world of coming judgment while offering God's free gift of salvation through an open door.

DINOSAUR DEN

DRAGON THEATER

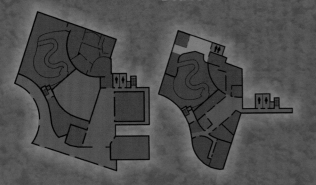

One of the questions Ken is frequently asked deals with dinosaurs: how do dinosaurs fit with the Bible? Of course, the Creation Museum had to deal with the answer to this not-so-difficult topic. And what better way than to include life-size sculptures of a variety of dinosaurs to illustrate the point that man and dinosaurs lived side-by-side from the beginning?

The Dinosaur Den was not completed for opening day; it was finished and opened to the public on July 4, 2007. This space was created as a place to feature dinosaurs and house some of Buddy's sculpted dinosaurs.

Many of Buddy's dinosaurs were refurbished and remodeled prior to being placed in the museum.

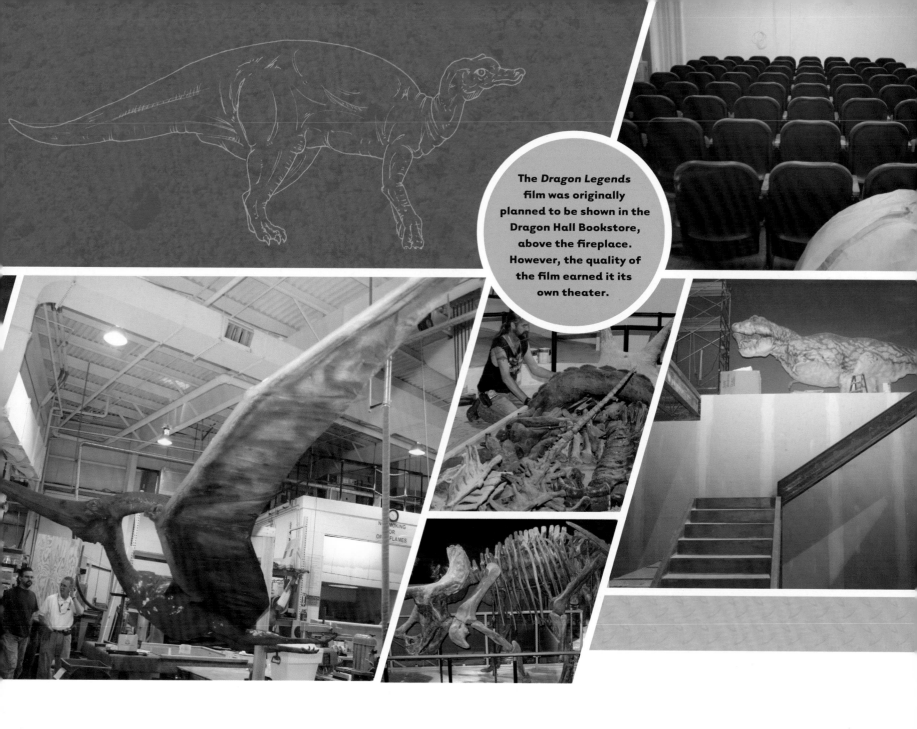

The *Dragon Legends* film was originally planned to be shown in the Dragon Hall Bookstore, above the fireplace. However, the quality of the film earned it its own theater.

LAKESIDE GRILL

The construction of the Lakeside Grill and adjacent bathrooms began before the museum opened, but construction was suspended during opening summer. Guests and staff often asked what the plans were for the partially completed space. The grill finally opened on June 27, 2008. Guests now have another space to dine, relieving some of the summer's long lines in Noah's Café.

Ministry staff volunteered to stain the chairs and tables that sit on the lakeside deck.

On busy days, we had numerous requests for additional facilities. The addition of these near the Grand Plaza and the ones by the Lakeside Grill addressed this concern.

PETTING ZOO

From the beginning, we wanted to build a petting zoo to provide another place where families with young children could have fun and be entertained, while at the same time learning something about creation and God's Word. The Petting Zoo opened on May 23, 2008. It was the featured new venue for our one-year anniversary.

A zorse and zonkey joined more traditional animals in the zoo.

...ATION MUSEUM PETTING ZOO

GRAND OPENING

May 23, 2008

PETTING Z
GRAND OP
May 23, 20

Who is Answers in Genesis?

Answers in Genesis worldwide headquarters—
near the Cincinnati International Airport

When we believe the Bible's literal history—including its teaching on geology, biology, anthropology, paleontology, and astronomy—we can logically defend it without compromising its theology, which proclaims salvation through faith in our Creator and Savior Jesus Christ.

It is our mission to teach Christians and non-Christians that the Bible makes sense of our world and culture today, and that we have logical, reliable answers to a skeptical world's most-asked questions such as:

- Is there really a God?

- Why is there death and suffering?

- What really happened to the dinosaurs?

- Where did Cain get his wife?

- Where did the races come from?

- How can I spend eternity in heaven?

Teaching Outreaches

With more than 10 speakers, we are reaching hundreds of thousands of young people and adults at teaching meetings around the world! Over 350 meetings are held each year with scores of meetings specially arranged for young people . . . equipping all ages to understand and defend the truth and authority of the Bible from the very first verse!

Answers Worldwide

Providing translated resources and teaching, *Answers Worldwide* is the missionary arm of Answers in Genesis. With over 100 translation projects, its purpose is to provide the "global Christian" with answers for his faith (1 Peter 3:15) and to expose the world to the Creator God of the Bible.

Dr. David Crandall

Creation Museum

Opened in May 2007, the one-of-a-kind Creation Museum near the Cincinnati Airport attracted 400,000 people from around the world in its first year alone. It is a visual walk through history—according to the Bible and not evolution—that features world-class exhibits, a planetarium, four unique theaters, and an effective presentation of the gospel.

Web

Our award-winning website is one of the most popular Christian internet destinations in the world—averaging 30,000 different guests per day! Use AnswersInGenesis.org as your primary source for relevant, reliable, Bible-upholding information!

Radio

The *Answers . . . with Ken Ham* radio program equips listeners to defend the Christian faith! We broadcast on over 900 radio stations worldwide every weekday. Ken Ham and other AiG speakers have also become popular talkshow guests (e.g., CNN, Fox News) on creation vs. evolution issues.

Resources

We create and distribute new faith-building and evangelistic materials. An average of 40 new books, DVDs, and magazines are released each year!

It is our passion to proclaim to all who will listen that the Bible's history is true!